The wondrous world of CATS

The wondrous world of CATS

Text by DAVID GIBBON

Designed and produced by TED SMART

Photography
© Colour Library International Ltd.

First published in Great Britain in 1976
by Colour Library International Ltd.

Printed by OFSA Milano
and bound by L.E.G.O. Vicenza Italy

Display and text filmsetting by
Focus Photoset Ltd.,
134 Clerkenwell Road, London EC1R 5DL.

ISBN 0 8148 0668 6

Enquiries should be sent to:
Leon Amiel Publisher
31, W. 46th Street
New York
New York 10036

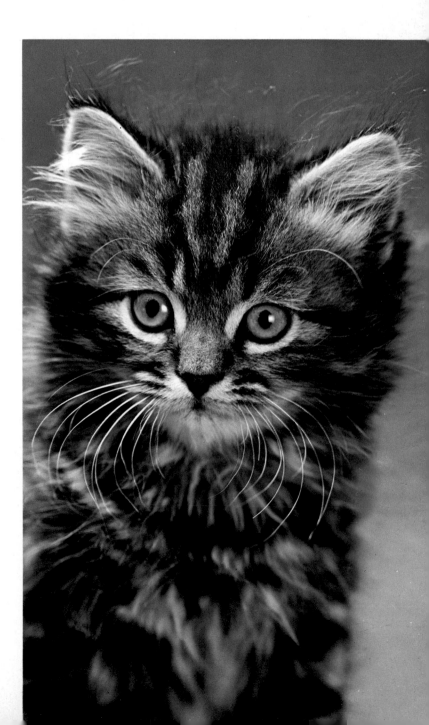

(LEFT)
Long haired tabby & white kitten

(RIGHT)
Long haired tabby & white kitten

Text books, encyclopaedias and such like have a rather dismissive way of dealing with subjects we have a great interest in which, whilst being entirely factual, leave us with rather a flat feeling. As an example of what I mean, I find in such a book, under the heading 'Cats' the following definition: 'the generic name for all quadrupeds of the Digitigrade section of the carnivorous order, from the lion down to the domestic cat'. There is no doubting the scientific truth of the description but, by its very nature a book such as the one in which I found this description has to generalise, and if there is one thing you cannot generalise about it is cats!

(TOP)
3 Chinchilla kittens

(LEFT BOTTOM)
Orange eyed white Persian

(RIGHT BOTTOM)
Chinchilla Cat

I do not propose, in The Wondrous World of Cats, to go into the question of the evolution of the 'Digitigrade section of the carnivorous order', or into the relationship between the large cats, lions and tigers, and the domestic cat. The purpose of this book is to deal primarily with the domestic cat and its relationship with us, the people who think we own one of these graceful creatures.

It has been argued that man has a subconscious feeling of inferiority, a fear of rejection, in his relationships with his fellow men and that this is one of the prime reasons why he seeks the companionship of animals with which to share his life. Whether this is true or not it is certainly the case that, however rejected he may be, (and sometimes with justification) if he has an animal, a pet dog or cat, waiting for him at home then he knows that here at least he will not find such rejection. Once inside his own home he knows that his companion will accept him for what he is, without question. It is also true to say, surely, that man has a great desire to feel needed and, whilst he looks for fulfilment of this desire in, primarily, his fellows he

(TOP)
Long haired cream, long haired ginger &
short haired ginger kittens

(BOTTOM)
Long haired blue cream kitten

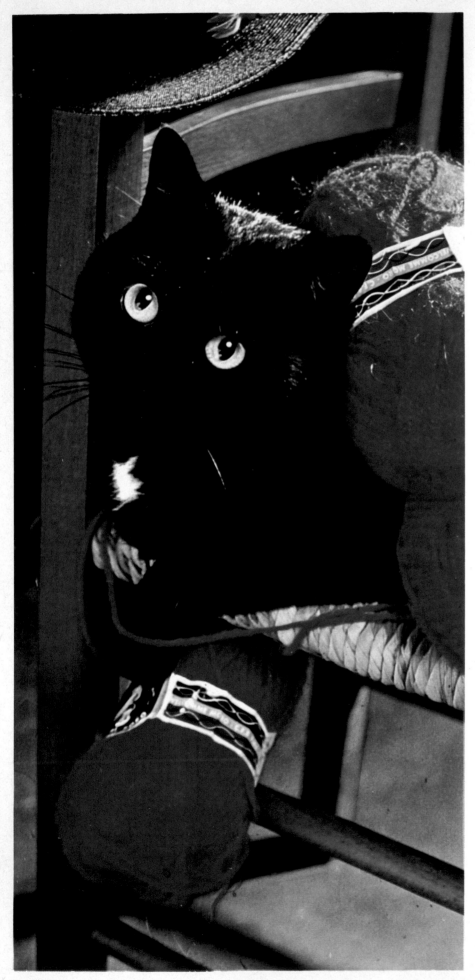

knows that he is not unique amongst them in this respect and that he is just one of millions all sharing the same need. Such knowledge alone, whether consciously considered or not, is sufficient to promote a feeling, however vague, of insecurity, and to tend to make him look elsewhere for reinforcement of this basic need. That he finds, at least in part, fulfilment in the companionship of the animals he takes into his home is amply demonstrated by the long history of such associations and the enormous number of such pets that are to be found in almost every country in the world.

Having established at least some of the reasons for the popularity of pets as companions we now find that there is another division; that of 'dog people' and 'cat people'. This is not to say that there are not many people who find both species attractive and, in fact, may keep one or more of each, nor would it be true to say that those who keep only a dog do not like cats, or vice-versa. Almost invariably, ownership of a pet animal infers a liking for animals generally. Nevertheless there are many people for whom the cat is an ideal companion, just as there are dog owners for the same reason.

The differences between dog ownership and cat ownership are fundamental to the differences between the animals themselves. A dog requires far more 'looking after' in day to day living than a cat and is therefore far more demanding of time and attention. Unless great muddy footprints are to spread throughout the house a dog, when it has been out in the garden during muddy weather, has to have its feet wiped clean. It will come to you asking to be taken for a walk and will show a keen interest in visitors! A cat, on the other hand, will tend to look after its own needs to a far greater extent and, whilst it can be very affectionate, will bestow such affection with an almost regal air. A dog can very easily be trained to perform all kinds of tricks which it will perform to order. A cat, although equally intelligent, very soon indicates that the learning of tricks is beneath its dignity and will watch you performing all sorts of

(LEFT)
Short haired black cat

(RIGHT)
Short haired black cat

6

antics in an effort to get it to do something, until you begin to feel rather foolish and the cat walks away with a disdainful air! When a cat decides, for its own good reasons, that it will emulate dog like behaviour by, say, begging, it will do it of its own volition with superb grace and contemptuous ease.

Except in a very few instances such as farm animals and perhaps in some shops, cats particularly are no longer kept primarily for their prowess as hunters. At one time there was hardly a home without its 'mouser', but then, there was hardly a home without its mice! In those days cats were almost essential in keeping down the vermin population, and they certainly earned their keep. This natural hunting instinct is something that can distress a number of people. The problem seems to be that, because a person owns a cat it generally follows, as has been mentioned, that they are fond of all animals and the sight of a cat apparently torturing a small animal or bird quite needlessly is something that appears, on the surface, to be an extremely unpleasant and cruel trait.

The fact is that a cat is a hunter, however, and what is seen as needless cruelty is, more likely, simply the cat practising its skills in the only way it can. That cats take pride in their ability as hunters may be seen in the way they will often 'present' their prey to their masters or mistresses by carefully leaving the corpses outside their door! To then scold the cat for taking pride in what it is, a hunter, is as pointless as scolding a dog for guarding its home against strangers.

Rather earlier in this book I remarked about "people who think we own one of these graceful creatures". This was not a slip of the pen, or typewriter! It has always seemed to me, when visiting or talking to cat owners, that it is a very valid comment. There is no doubt, with dog owners, that they are the owners of the dog, but with cats it is a very different matter. You only have to look at the way a cat walks into its home and the familiarity with which it treats it and the occupants to understand that, whilst

(TOP)
Short haired black cat

(BOTTOM)
Short haired orange & white cat

(RIGHT)
Long haired white kitten

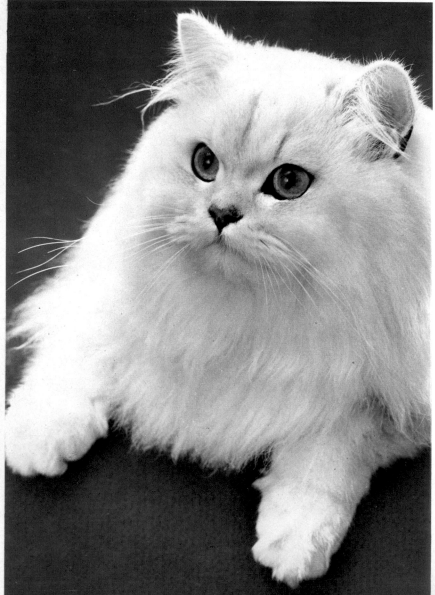

the owner may think he or she owns the cat, the cat is under no such misapprehension and gives every indication of not being owned by anybody; it is either a mutual arrangement or nothing!

Cat ownership does not require the purchase of a licence. It is not easy, therefore, to arrive at an exact figure for the cat population at any one time. Nevertheless, the best estimates seem to indicate that cat ownership is increasing whilst, at the same time, dog ownership is decreasing slightly. This does not, of course, mean that dogs are no longer popular. What it does highlight is that present social and economic conditions, amongst other factors, are more conducive to the ownership of cats than dogs. So many of the small houses in our cities have now disappeared, to be replaced by high rise blocks of flats, in which the ownership of dogs is almost invariably discouraged if not forbidden and, in any case, is inconvenient for both the dog and the owner. The cost of feeding all but the smallest dogs is considerably higher than the cost of keeping a cat as many owners of large dogs have found, to their surprise. In such situations, those of us for whom the companionship of a pet is something we do not want to forego, find that a cat is the ideal answer. Apart from feeding, and affection a cat can very largely be left to its own devices, something which can be very important if the owner is out at work all day, and in return can, and invariably will, give the greatest amount of pleasure.

The cat has always had something of an air of mystery about it. Even its origins are obscure. It is obviously related to the 'big cats' but the domestic cat was certainly well known to the ancient Egyptians, to whom they rendered great service by helping to control the rats and mice that infested their grain stores. It is also known that the Egyptians worshipped the cat as divine, and were, as far as is known, the only people to do so. It would be a mistake to make too much of this, however, as the Egyptians treated many other animals as divine and most of their Gods had some animal characteristic attributed to them, the

(TOP)
Short haired tortoiseshell & white kitten

(BOTTOM)
Chinchilla cat

jackal and the cobra being but two of the more obvious examples. Many animals were mummified by the Egyptians, including cats and mice; the latter presumably to provide food for the cat on its journey to the other world!

The deification that the Egyptians afforded the cat proved to have disastrous consequences for the animal during the middle ages in Europe. The cat was, by this time, firmly established as a domestic pet but its ancestry of Godliness, and therefore its association with good and evil had by no means been forgotten. These were very superstitious times and anything unusual was very quickly pronounced to be witchcraft or the work of the Devil. There were other factors that also worked to the disadvantage of the cat. Inevitably a large number of the women who were regarded as witches were older women living alone, almost as recluses, and it was extremely likely that they would keep one or more cats as companions. Coupled with this was the cat's natural air of mystery, the eyes, the silent movements and the habit of staring at people as though assessing them. Cats have always produced an allergy in some people. Properly known as aileurophobia, it usually takes the form of causing sneezing, and breathing difficulties, in those afflicted – even when the cat is nowhere in sight. To a superstitious people, beset by fears of witches and demons, all these things must have very quickly convinced them that the cat, far from being an ordinary animal, must be possessed of supernatural powers! The consequence of all this was that the poor cat was hounded and persecuted every bit as much, if not more, than the unfortunate owners. Many cats were put to death along with their mistresses, and many more were chased and killed, or burnt as sacrifices, by mindless mobs.

Even today cats, particularly black cats, figure prominently, at least as cut-outs or drawings, in Hallowe'en celebrations and there is hardly a story published for children in which a witch appears that does not also feature a black cat as her 'familiar'. Given that cats, for entirely the wrong reasons,

(RIGHT)
Short haired tortoiseshell & white kitten

(OVERLEAF)
Long haired tabby & white kittens

were, and to some extent still are, associated with witchcraft, it is not difficult to imagine why it is the black cat that figures so strongly in this context. In those 'dark' ages lighting was either non-existent, or of very poor quality, and witchcraft and sorcery were invariably associated with night-time. In such a situation a black cat would hardly be seen at all, except for the eyes which, with their retinas reflecting the light of torches, would appear to shine with what the on-lookers could easily convince themselves was an unearthly glow. To be fair, the sight of a black cat with shining eyes and arched back, spitting furiously in the half light, is a rather unnerving sight at the best of times and to those ill-educated people it must have been quite terrifying!

The ability that cats have, in the minds of many people, to evoke a feeling of supernatural forces or even, sometimes, of terror – which may well be a leftover from those dark ages – is something that film producers have put to good use, many times over, in the making of particular films. Whilst this is very understandable from the film maker's point of view, and he is, after all, merely triggering something in the minds of the viewers, it seems rather unfair on the poor cat! A great number of those who declare a dis-liking for cats in general must have such feelings reinforced, if not occasion-ally introduced, by the dramatic uses to which cats are put in books, theatres and cinemas. That such feelings are quite irrational is obvious to anyone who owns a cat or knows the animals well. A cat is simply a cat, no more, no less. It does not seek to imitate anything and all its actions are purely catlike.

The popularly held belief that 'a cat has nine lives' means that enor-mous luck is attributed to the animal at the expense of recognizing the truth of the matter; that the cat is possessed of extraordinary reflexes coupled with

(TOP LEFT)
Short haired tabby kittens

(BOTTOM LEFT)
4 Long haired tabby & 1 tortoiseshell kittens

(TOP)
Short haired ginger & Long haired blue cream kittens

(BOTTOM)
Long haired ginger & Long haired cream kittens

superb coordination between mind and muscle. It is this that allows them to escape from all sorts of seemingly impossible situations rather than mere luck. The remarkable thing about the cat's physical prowess is just how little real exercise they seem to need in order to stay in such good condition. Even after long periods of inactivity reflexes appear to remain unimpaired and judgement and timing are as good as ever.

Because of their abilities as hunters and their air of independence, it is sometimes thought that cats can fend entirely for themselves, living on the food that they catch and finding shelter wherever it is available. This, however, is quite incorrect. The domestic cat has been domesticated for far too long for it to be able to look after itself completely. Cats need people and a comfortable home. They need to be fed a proper diet and to have a warm place to sleep, and they need affection. Most people who have travelled to any extent on the continent will have seen examples of the pitifully thin and unkempt homeless cats that try to support themselves, sometimes with equally emaciated kittens, and will know how obviously necessary it is to look after a cat properly.

There are a number of anomalies concerning cats, as indeed there are with so many things in life. They are themselves creatures of great contradictions; at times apparently lazy in the extreme and yet capable of great athleticism; giving every indication of being totally uncaring about the humans with whom they share their lives at one moment, and curling up on someone's lap, purring with contentment, at the next. In many parts of England a black cat is considered to be lucky and appears on postcards and so on, together with a horseshoe, as a symbol of good luck. Only in a few counties are they thought to be unlucky, whereas in the United States the reverse is largely the case.

(TOP)
Long haired cream & Long haired ginger kittens

(BOTTOM)
Blue Persian kitten

(RIGHT)
Long haired orange eyed white kitten

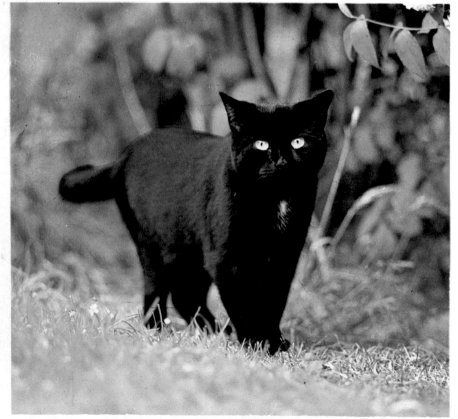

It might be thought that cats rarely meet each other except to either mate or fight and yet there are well documented instances of them using a common meeting place to do neither of these things but simply spend time in the company of other cats, apparently enjoying some kind of social get-together!

Although cats, as I have mentioned already, are thought of as mysterious and, in some contexts, sinister they are also the most popular cartoon, comic, and pantomime characters. Felix the Cat, Korky, Sylvester, Puss-in-Boots, and Dick Whittington's cat seldom fail to find great appreciation and affection from younger readers and audiences. Perhaps the reason is that, as children, we find very few things or creatures mysterious or sinister but simply accept them for what they

(TOP)
Short haired black cat

(BOTTOM)
Short haired black cat

appear to be, whereas when we grow up we start to read, and to listen to older people, and then realise that we were wrong all the time! We are all obviously creatures of our own civilizations and, as we get older we simply accept its conventions without question. Little girls are not expected to like frogs, toads, mice, or insects and so they almost invariably develop a fear and dislike of them, whilst little boys develop the reverse characteristics, they are expected to like messing about in ponds, hunting for tadpoles, have a matchbox or two in their pockets containing various insects and so, by and large, that is exactly what they do!

People in all walks of life own cats. There is, however, a quite distinct leaning, on the part of writers, poets, actors, and even politicians, towards cat ownership. Apparently Doctor Johnson was very fond of his pet cat, which must have proved rather a trial at times for Boswell who was, it is understood, allergic to them! Possibly one of the major attractions that cats hold for such people is that they are so undemanding; they allow you to get on with what you are doing without interruption and they seem to have an air of contemplation about them

(TOP)
Short haired tabby & white cat

(BOTTOM)
Short haired tabby kittens

which may be well suited to a particular type of person.

As is common with most animals, cats are at their most irresistible when they are very young. It is very hard indeed not to find a kitten appealing and this inevitably, as with puppies, leads to a lot of tragedy. It seems quite astonishing to me that so many people will buy a kitten, simply because they find it so appealing and not give any consideration to whether they really want a cat or not. They find that the adorable little kitten turns into a grown cat, decide that, after all, they do not really want a grown animal and the responsibilities that ownership implies, and the wretched animal finds itself out on the streets, unwanted and uncared for. Both dogs and cats suffer appallingly in this way, and quite needlessly, if only a little thought was given before the animal was purchased. I do not personally think that the issuing of licenses would do a great deal to alleviate the problem; it certainly has not, so far as can be seen, helped greatly in preventing the same thing happening with dogs. Probably one real answer would be to make the initial acquisition of the kitten that much more difficult by not allowing cats or dogs to be sold except by registered breeders who could, perhaps, operate some kind of follow-up procedure, or at least make sure, before any animal was handed over, that the prospective owners were fully aware of what they were embarking upon in deciding to become animal owners. A long term solution that has often been suggested would be to embark on a programme of neutering a large proportion of the male cat population and thereby decrease, drastically, the numbers of unwanted kittens that are born.

When it is finally decided, hopefully after careful thought, that a kitten, and subsequently a cat, would be a desirable addition to the household there are several things that must be done. It is absolutely no use simply buying the kitten and taking it home without providing ample provision for its welfare in advance of its arrival. It is probable that this will be the first

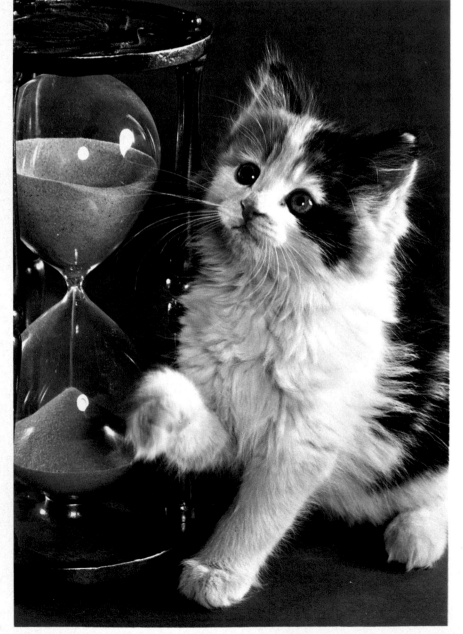

(TOP)
3 Short haired tabby kittens

(BOTTOM)
Long haired tortoiseshell & white kitten

(RIGHT)
Long haired tabby & white cat

time that the new kitten has been away from its mother and her other kittens, and it will understandably feel strange, and lonely. It will be in totally unfamiliar surroundings and it is of prime importance that it gets used to these new surroundings and learns to accept them as its new home. All kittens require a warm, draught-free bed to sleep in; young kittens are particularly susceptible to any draughts. Obviously food will have to be available and this should be finely chopped meat or fish rather than tinned cat food. The kitten will be greedy, as are most young animals, and it is much better, therefore, to provide three or four small meals a day rather than letting it eat its fill at one sitting. Most, but not all, cats like milk, so water may have to be tried if the kitten appears to find milk not to its liking. Cats are instinctively clean animals but they are also taught cleanliness by their mothers. Should a kitten prove not to be completely house trained it is usually a fairly simple matter to teach it.

All kittens should be seen by a veterinary surgeon, preferably before it is taken home, but if this is not possible, then certainly as soon afterwards as it can be arranged, so that it may be examined for any possible ailments. There will also be vaccinations required, which the veterinary surgeon will advise on.

It seems surprising that it was only just over a hundred years ago, in 1871, that the first official cat show took place, in the Crystal Palace. Since that time Cat Clubs, Cat Fanciers' Associations, and Cat Societies are to be found throughout the world. There are clubs catering for particular breeds of cats, such as the Siamese Cat Club, the Black and White Cat Club, the Brown Tabby Society, and many, many more. It is not always necessary for a cat to come from a long line of champions in order that it should make a successful show cat. Cats which have

(LEFT)
2 Long haired Cream kittens

(TOP)
Long haired ginger kitten & Long haired Cream kitten

(BOTTOM)
2 Long haired ginger kittens

(OVERLEAF)
2 Long haired tabby & white kittens

23

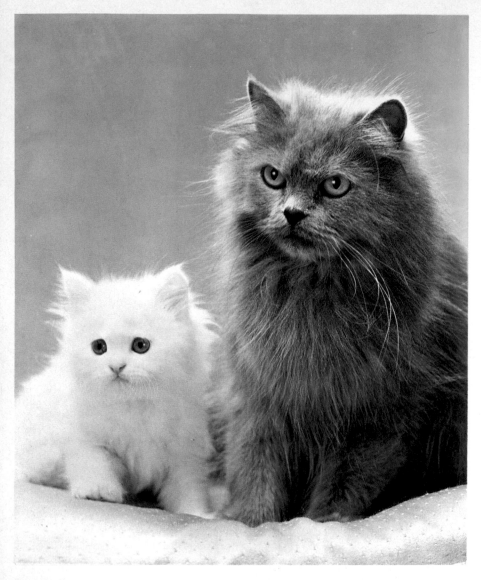

no particular pedigree have won classes at shows, providing that their markings are well defined, eyes the correct colour, head well shaped and so on for the class for which they are entered, usually 'Any Other Variety'.

Most people who own a cat will probably never want to enter it for a show, however, as they will be perfectly happy to simply share their home, and their life, with the companion of their choice.

The Faithful Cat

Whenever the idea of a faithful companion, waiting for its master or mistress, is considered, it usually conjures up a picture of a dog, patiently anticipating the sound of the familiar voice or footstep. This is perfectly true, of course. Dogs are much more demonstrative in their greetings than are cats. Nevertheless, it would be wrong to think that cats are not interested in the absence, or impending return, of their human companion. I'm sure that most of us have heard of cats waiting, sometimes at the door, or even at the garden gate, ready to offer a 'welcome home' greeting. I recently heard of a cat that goes much further than this and, in fact, behaves very much more like a dog in this respect. The cat lives in a small village and the master travels by train from the local station each day. The cat appears to know, each day, the time that its master will be returning and, at the appointed time, sets out for the station, some two miles distant, and waits for him. This particular cat can quite easily pick him out from all the other returning passengers, and does so regularly! Most of the local people know the cat, a Siamese, and it is something of a local celebrity.

Such behaviour is, of course, rather out of the ordinary but, there is no question that, in a happy home, a cat will always be pleased to see its owner, whether it acts in an outwardly demonstrative manner or not.

(TOP)
White Persian kitten & Blue Persian Cat

(BOTTOM)
Orange eyed white Persian cats

(RIGHT)
Short haired cream & short haired blue cream kittens

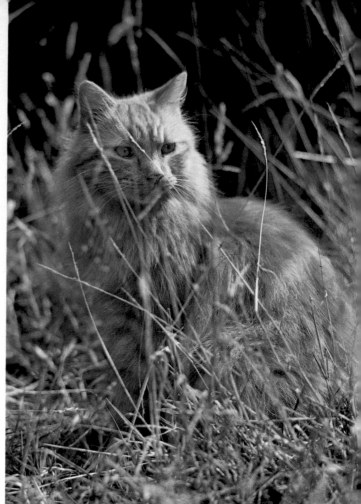

(ABOVE)
Short haired tabby cat

(RIGHT)
Long haired ginger cat

(BOTTOM)
Short haired ginger & white cat

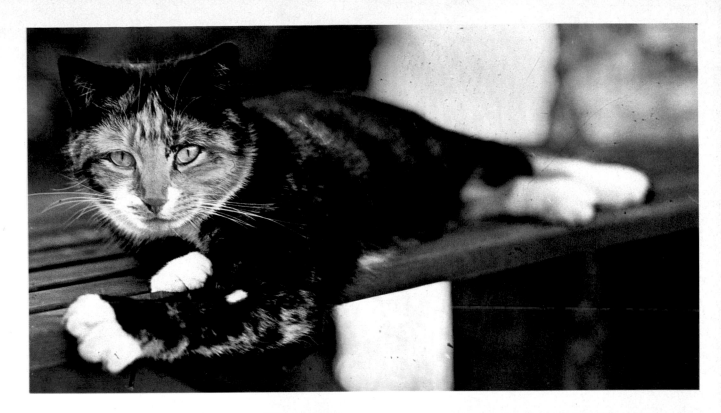

The Cat's good health!

Not an invitation to raise your glass and toast the well-being of your feline companion! Rather, a few words on the general health and fitness of cats.

In general, cats are very healthy animals providing they are well cared for with regard to food, grooming and a comfortable home. It is, however, essential that a cat is vaccinated against feline infectious enteritis, usually at two to three months old. This particular disease is extremely infectious and, even if symptoms are recognized early and treatment started immediately, it is almost always fatal. Obviously the best person to offer advice, to carry out the vaccination and subsequent 'booster' doses, is the vet. It is therefore important to choose a vet in the area, preferably not too far away, in case of emergencies, and who will, from the outset, have a complete record of all treatment given to the cat and will be in an ideal position to treat the animal, knowing its full medical history.

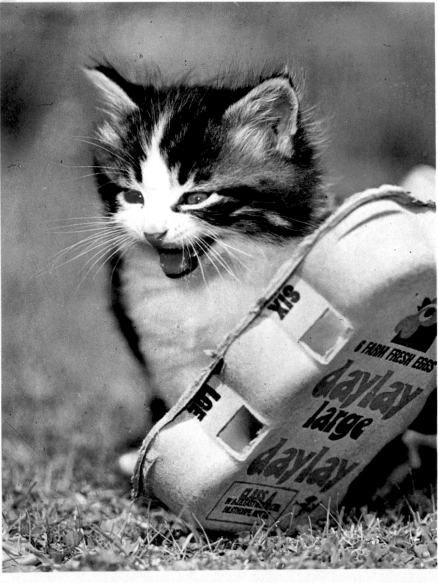

(TOP)
Short haired tortoiseshell cat

(BOTTOM)
Long haired tabby & white kitten

Unless it is seriously intended that the cat will breed and that resulting kittens will be properly catered for, it is wise to have the cat neutered. This should take place before six months but again, the vet will advise on the exact timing. In the case of male kittens the operation is very simple indeed. For female kittens it is a little more complex and takes rather longer but, as with the male, the operation has now become very much routine, is quite safe and the kitten will suffer the very minimum discomfort.

In addition to eye infections, the symptoms of which are usually readily

(TOP)
Short haired ginger & Long haired cream kittens

(BOTTOM)
Long haired black, Long haired tortoiseshell, Long haired black, Long haired tabby kittens

(TOP RIGHT)
Long haired ginger, short haired ginger, Long haired cream kittens

(BOTTOM RIGHT)
Long haired cream kitten

(OVERLEAF)
3 White Persian kittens

31

apparent; closing of the eye, redness, watering etc., obvious injuries such as cuts, grazes or bites which might lead to more serious problems and may result in an abscess are, again, best dealt with by the vet. It is difficult to bandage a cat's wound successfully for two reasons. In the first place the cat has a very loose skin, something which will be readily apparent to anyone who has tried to hold a cat firmly against its will! Secondly, the cat, like most other animals, does not like bandages or dressings and will frequently try to remove them, sometimes even to the extent of taking out stitches!

Simple ailments, particularly worms – both tape and round – and fleas or lice, are comparatively easy to treat and control. There are many preparations on the market to deal with such problems but it is of the utmost importance that only products of a reputable make, and specifically designed for cats, should be used. It cannot be stressed too strongly that unsuitable medicines of any sort should never be given to cats. This is particularly true of preparations designed for humans. Even a simple aspirin, usually the first thing to be taken by people for a great variety of aches and pains, can prove fatal to a cat.

Probably the wisest thing to end by saying is – if in doubt about any aspect of the cat's health, then consult the only person properly trained and equipped to deal with it – the vet.

Cats and kittens

Unless the owner of a female cat, or 'queen' has had her 'neutered' to make her incapable of having a family, the time will come when the cat will obey her natural instincts and seek the company of a mate. At this time she will want to spend her time out in the open as much as possible, and it is very difficult indeed to make sure that she remains indoors, or under supervision when taking exercise. The most likely, and obvious, result is that the cat will become pregnant. The usual gestation period for a cat is about sixty days and, when giving birth to her kittens, she will normally be able to look after herself quite adequately. It is wise, however, to make a nesting place, or bed, for her which is dark, secluded and, above all, draught-free.

Tabby & white cat & litter of kittens

This latter requirement is of the utmost importance for the welfare of the newly born kittens as they are particularly susceptible to draughts. The bed should be provided with some form of disposable material, even paper will do, to cover her blanket so that it can be destroyed once the kittens have been born.

The number of kittens in a litter can, of course, vary from cat to cat but five or six kittens would be a reasonable average. Should any of the kittens be born dead they must be removed straight away and disposed of. In the event that any of the kittens are not wanted they should on no account be simply taken away and drowned. It used to be quite common for this to happen but drowning causes quite unnecessary suffering, whatever the age of the creature, and it is far preferable to take the kittens to a Veterinarian and have them painlessly put to sleep. If none of the kittens are born alive for some reason then, again, it would be wise to take the mother to the Vet as she will be producing milk for her offspring which will not be used, and he will be able to remedy the problem.

Hopefully, of course, the kittens will all be alive and healthy and will be destined for good homes when they are old enough to leave their mother.

When they are first born the kittens will be both blind and deaf, and very helpless. Nevertheless they will immediately start looking for food from their mother and will be perfectly well looked after by her. It should be borne in mind that the mother will require considerably more nourishment than normal during the time that she is feeding her family and this should take the form of good, protein rich food, such as white fish, chicken, rabbit, liver etc., and of course milk. It is generally supposed that all cats love milk but, surprisingly, many actually prefer water to cow's milk. This may possibly be due to the fact that a very large proportion of cow's milk is, in fact, water and it does not have the

(LEFT)
Long haired tabby & white kitten

(TOP)
2 White Persian kittens

(BOTTOM)
2 Long haired ginger kittens with a Long haired cream kitten

nutritional value of either goat's milk or tinned milk, particularly for a nursing mother or for a kitten being weaned.

After giving birth to her kittens the queen will require rest and it would be wise not to disturb either her or her kittens, certainly for the first few hours after the birth has taken place.

At about a week old the kittens will start to open their eyes and take notice of their surroundings. They are still, however, very delicate little creatures and they should be handled as little as possible. After a further two weeks the kittens will probably start to crawl around and from then on they should become stronger, and more adventurous, quite quickly. It is at this time that weaning can be started, remembering that kittens, like puppies, are naturally greedy and it is wise to give them the right amount of food, and no more, rather than allow them to gorge, and make themselves ill!

Cats are naturally clean creatures and the new mother will both pass on this instinct and train her offspring to be clean. When the cats start to wander around, therefore, it would be as well to provide a box filled with sand or earth which can be changed every day until the kittens are ready to venture out of doors.

Whatever the breeds of cat that make up the parentage of the new kittens; whether they are pure bred or not, the kittens themselves will almost certainly be quite adorable. Their mischievousness, zest for life and curiosity about everything that goes on around them makes them very hard indeed to resist, and makes parting with them, when the time comes for them to go, hopefully, to good homes, something that is never less than difficult.

(TOP)
A Long haired cream kitten and 2 Long haired ginger kittens

(BOTTOM)
A Long haired blue cream and a Long haired cream kitten

(RIGHT)
Cream Persian kitten

38

Cats on show

The first cat show was held at the Crystal Palace, near London, in 1871. Since that time both cat shows and cat societies, often devoted to one particular breed, have flourished. Nevertheless it is true to say that, compared with the vast population of cats throughout the world, the number that are actually shown is relatively small. Apart from cat breeders, to whom the winning of prizes is of obvious importance, most of the people who enter their cats for shows do so very much for the fun and pleasure they get out of the experience. The fact that a cat can be entered for every show for which it is eligible, without ever coming near to winning a prize of any sort, should, of course, in no way diminish it in the eyes of its owner, to whom it will remain the most beautiful cat in the world, and this is as it should be.

(LEFT) White Persian kitten

(TOP) Short haired cream cat and kitten

(BOTTOM) 2 Long haired blue cream kittens

(OVERLEAF) Long haired tabby cat and kitten

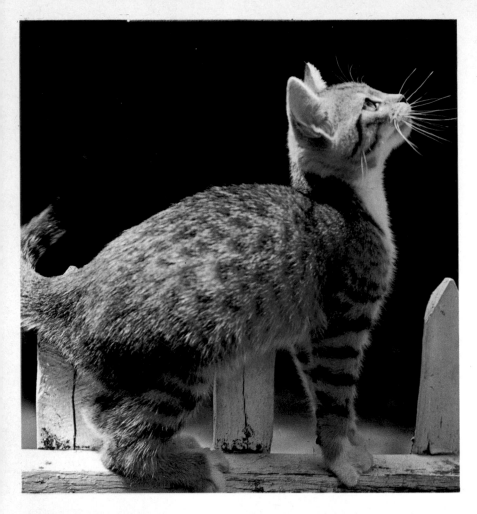

Every cat show, except those restricted to only one breed, have different sections for various breeds of cat and range in size, scope and importance from small local events to great shows such as the Olympia National Cat Show. Before entering any cat for a show, whether local or national, it is wise to read carefully all the conditions of entry. With 'serious' shows it is usual for there to be insistence that the cat is registered with the appropriate body and, in all cases, proof is required that the cat has been vaccinated and is healthy. Obviously it would be disastrous if a cat suffering from some infectious disease were to come into contact with a large number of healthy animals and infect them. This was by no means unknown in the early days of cat shows, but is, happily, no longer a problem.

There are very many, and distinct, different breeds of cat but they are normally classified under four main headings; Long-haired or Persian, Short-haired (excluding Foreign), Foreign Short-haired (excluding Siamese), and Siamese. Within the first two groups particularly, there are a number of breeds that appear in both, the only real difference being that they have either long or short hair. Under Foreign Short-haired may be found some of the more exotic breeds, such as the Abyssinian, Russian, Burmese, Tonkanese, Havana etc., whilst under Siamese, which might be thought a fairly straightforward classification, there are now such varieties as Tabby-point, Tortoiseshell-point, Red-point as well as the, perhaps, more familiar Seal, Chocolate, Lilac and Blue-points.

In addition to all the recognized breeds of cat there are always sections covering 'any other colour', or 'any other variety'. If it is felt, therefore, that a cat does not fit into any of the distinct breeds there is no need to worry; who knows, perhaps a new trend will be set and a new classification introduced, in time, of which your cat could be the first champion!

(TOP)
Short haired tabby cat

(BOTTOM)
2 Short haired tabby cats

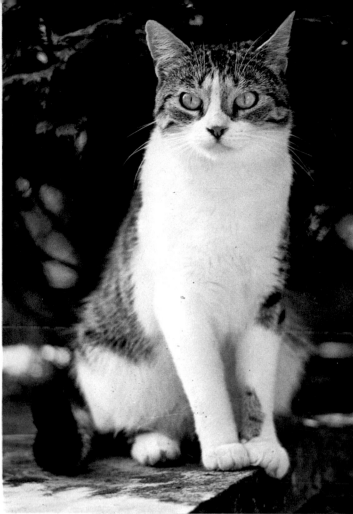

Cats in Photography

As has already been mentioned, cats, and particularly kittens, are tremendously appealing to look at. The fluffiness of the little animal, its big eyes and general air of inquisitiveness, coupled with the great vulnerability that is so apparent in any young creature, are all ingredients that have been put to exceedingly good purpose by publishers of postcards, greetings cards, calendars, chocolate boxes, and a great number of other commodities that rely on the eye of the prospective purchaser being attracted to the product. This, in turn, has obviously led to a considerable demand for really outstanding photographs, such as many that appear in this book. Whilst

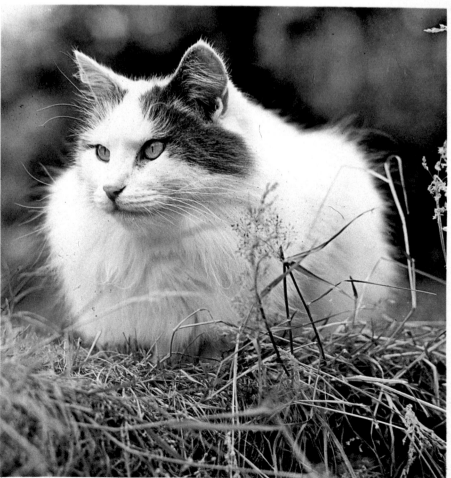

(TOP LEFT)
Short haired ginger tabby cat

(TOP RIGHT)
Short haired tabby and white cat

(BOTTOM)
Long haired blue and white cat

it is not too difficult to obtain a fairly passable snapshot of the family pet, good enough to be put in the album and shown to friends, when it comes to providing high quality colour photographs, with the cats or kittens carefully arranged into a pleasing composition that will be suitable for commercial purposes, then it is a very different story. A bowl of flowers, or some other still life arrangement may well be no easy task to set up but, once the elements of the picture are arranged to the photographer's satisfaction, they will at least stay put and give ample time for the photograph to be taken. Not so with kittens, or most other animals for that matter. A kitten, in particular, is very active, inquisitive, mischievous and, perhaps above all, self willed. Contrary to what anyone

(LEFT)
3 White Persian kittens

(TOP)
Short haired ginger kitten

(BOTTOM)
3 Long haired ginger kittens

(OVERLEAF)
Long haired blue cream kitten and White Persian kitten

47

may think, it is not really possible to scold a kitten, or punish it in any way, to make it cooperate with a photographer. It has to be a case of patience and then more patience, if necessary adapting the requirements of the photograph to the wishes of the kitten, rather than the other way around. A frightened kitten or cat will look unmistakeably either frightened or hostile in the finished work and no-one will want to use photographs that show this, so any attempt on the part of the photographer to try to impose his will too strongly will prove to be a complete waste of time.

(TOP)
2 White Persian kittens

(BOTTOM)
Long haired cream kitten and Long haired Blue cream kitten

(RIGHT)
Long haired Blue cream kitten

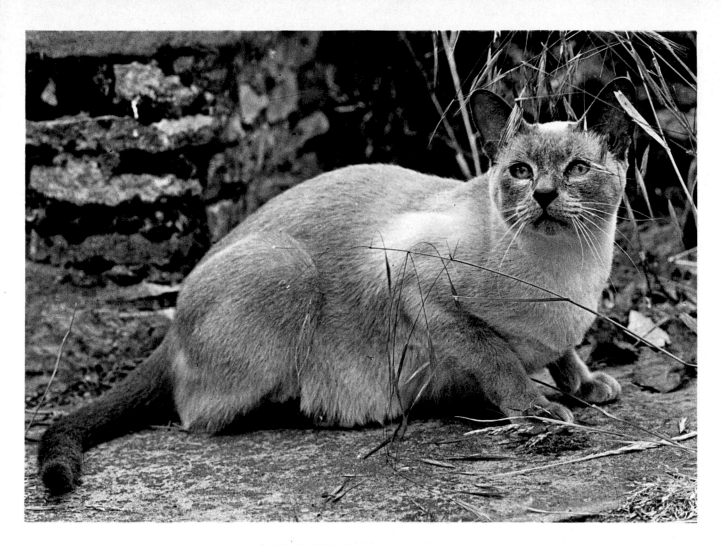

Most, if not all, successful animal photographers have a real understanding of, and with, the animals they use. It would be out of the question to simply take a kitten and place it in a pre-arranged setting and simply take the photograph. That is, unless that was precisely what the kitten wished to do at that particular time – not a very likely or frequent occurence! It is far more likely that the photographer will spend some considerable time playing with the kitten, getting to know it and gaining the animal's trust and confidence. Only after this point has been reached will he attempt to place the kitten in the setting he has arranged and watch the kitten's reactions. Often things do not quite work out in the way they have been planned.

(LEFT)
Seal Point Siamese cat

(TOP)
Blue point Siamese cat

(BOTTOM)
Blue point Siamese kittens

(OVERLEAF)
2 Seal point Siamese kittens

I have known occasions where the kitten has played for too long and, instead of a lively picture of an alert little animal, the result has been a photograph of a kitten fast asleep! Very appealing, but not what the photographer had in mind and it only remains for the original idea to be tried again when the kitten wakes up. Sometimes, of course, the kitten decides that it simply will not cooperate in any way and the whole idea has to be scrapped and replaced by something else.

It should be remembered that all the foregoing applies primarily to studio photography and that, in such work, large format cameras, of the type that require a dark cloth to be draped over the photographers' head in order that he may see the inverted image of the subject on a ground glass screen, are used. Whilst such cameras are capable of producing quite superb results and are essential in obtaining large transparencies or negatives they do, nevertheless, impose quite severe technical limitations on the photographer. Working at the very

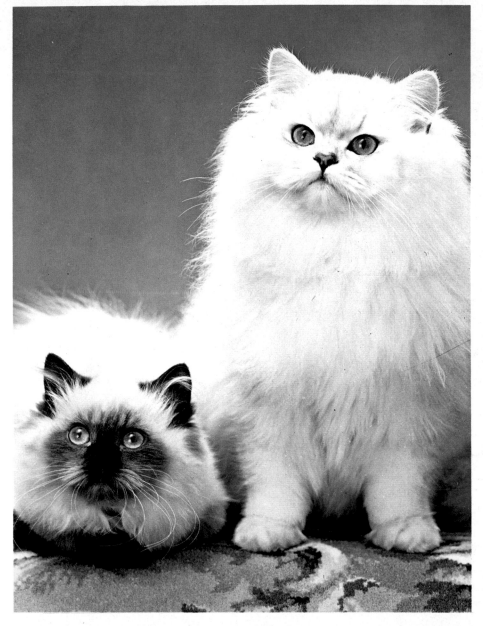

(TOP LEFT)
2 White Persian kittens and 2 Long haired tortoiseshell and white kittens

(BOTTOM LEFT)
3 Long haired black kittens

(TOP)
Sealpoint colourpoint cat and Chinchilla cat

(BOTTOM)
3 Long haired tabby kittens

57

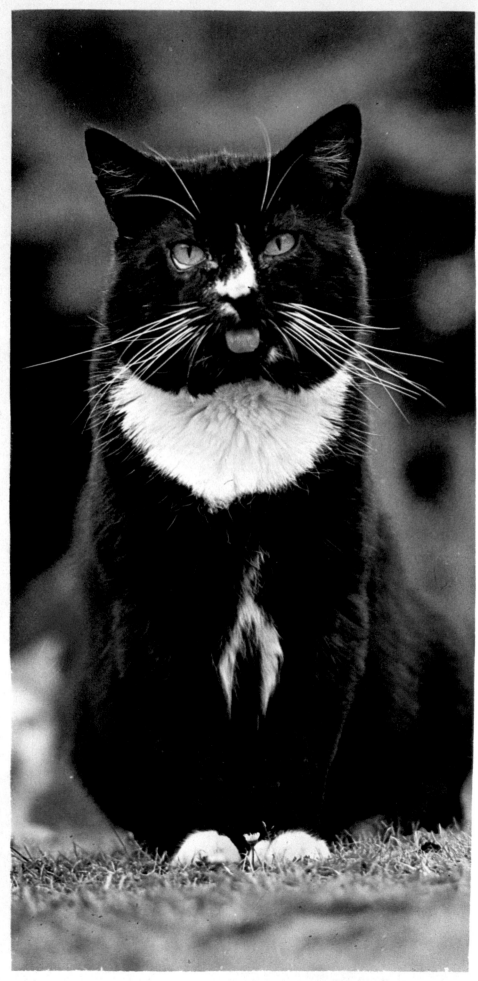

close distances necessary with a relatively small animal only a limited amount of the subject can be sharply focussed and, in the case of an animal which moves very quickly, this can prove to be an extremely difficult problem to overcome and usually necessitates the use of high powered flash equipment. In fact the kitten itself is rarely used for the preliminary focussing, this being done quite often by substituting a toy animal of the appropriate size which is removed when all has been made ready, the lighting and so on has been arranged, and is replaced, hopefully, by the kitten!

If I have succeeded in highlighting some of the difficulties that can be experienced in photographing a cat or kitten, in the studio, then the added complications of attempting to do the same but with two, three, four or more kittens in the one picture may be imagined! All the problems are multiplied by the number of animals, with the addition of trying to get them all to do what is wanted at the same time. Being present at such a time in an animal photographer's studio can be a quite hilarious experience for everyone – except, of course, for the photographer, who is probably wondering what perverse streak in his nature made him take up animal photography at all! With much perseverance, however, things do work out in the end and the feeling of achievement is quite considerable. Just how well they work out may be judged from the many photographs of two or more cats and kittens in this book, and such pictures are in themselves a great tribute to the skill and patience of the photographer concerned.

All Friends Together

In their wild state cats are natural hunters and do not make friends easily with other animals. This is perfectly understandable; another animal is either potential food to be hunted, and subsequently eaten, or is a threat to the cat's life and territory and is treated as such. If an animal falls into neither one nor the other of these categories

(LEFT)
Short haired black and white cat

(RIGHT)
Short haired tabby cat

then it is of no interest and is simply ignored. Territory is extremely important to most wild animals. This is not simply ecause the animal wants to have privacy, but for the very good reason that it is ensuring that an area is available when a family is born in which the offspring will be able to grow, and feed, in comparative security.

When an animal is domesticated and becomes the companion of human beings, to the extent of sharing a place in the family home, it still brings with it the instincts of the wild, to a greater or lesser degree. With cats, particularly, it is generally supposed that they do not take kindly to other aimals, except other cats, living in the same house. Whilst this is quite true in so far as a fully grown cat suddenly presented with, say, a dog as an additional household pet, would resent the intrusion strongly, it does

(LEFT)
2 White Persian kittens
(TOP)
3 Long haired ginger kittens
(BOTTOM)
Long haired tabby kitten

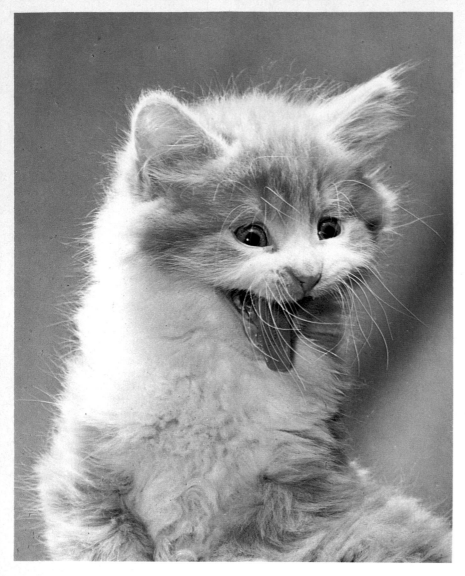

not mean cats will never live peacefully with dogs, rabbits or other animals. I'm quite sure that there are many recorded instances of cats even sharing their homes with birds, but I do feel that this might be stretching relationships a little too far as a normal course!

Should it be decided that, say, a cat and dog are wanted in a home, then it would obviously be the wisest course to get them as puppy and kitten respectively, so that they may grow up in one another's company from the outset. Failing such a possibility, it must be remembered that, in the same way as a child may feel resentment at a new brother or sister if it feels that enough attention is not being paid to it, or it feels, quite erroneously that it is not wanted as much as before the new arrival, this is very much the way an established pet will feel about a strange new companion. It is extremely important that the original pet, be it cat or dog, is made to feel wanted and loved as much as it ever was. In fact it would probably be wise to make even more of a fuss of it until it gets quite used to the new pet. Patience is the obvious ingredient in making sure that the new relationship achieves harmony. It must also be made quite clear, from the outset, that both pets have their own beds and food and drink bowls. Under no circumstances is it wise to allow certain behaviour from one animal, and to forbid it to the other. If the cat is allowed to lie on the settee, then it would be quite wrong to stop the dog from enjoying the same privilege, otherwise resentment is sure to build up.

Given the right amount of patience, understanding, firmness and tact, there is no reason at all why different animals, supposedly implacable enemies, should not be the best of friends. There is something particularly charming about such friendships and the owner, of course, gets the best of both worlds in having two different pets to make a fuss of and, in turn, to make a fuss of him or her.

(TOP)
Long haired ginger and white kitten

(BOTTOM)
2 Long haired tabby kittens

(RIGHT)
Long haired tortoiseshell and white kitten

(OVERLEAF)
Blue cream kittens